A Still Place

A Still Place

✦

One Woman's Journey Home

Nancy J. Lankston

iUniverse, Inc.

New York Lincoln Shanghai

A Still Place
One Woman's Journey Home

Copyright © 2005 by Nancy J. Lankston

iUniverse books may be ordered through booksellers or by contacting:

iUniverse
2021 Pine Lake Road, Suite 100
Lincoln, NE 68512
www.iuniverse.com
1-800-Authors (1-800-288-4677)

ISBN-13: 978-0-595-37757-2 (pbk)
ISBN-13: 978-0-595-82132-7 (ebk)
ISBN-10: 0-595-37757-2 (pbk)
ISBN-10: 0-595-82132-4 (ebk)

Printed in the United States of America

For David
My partner, my love and my friend
You have shown me what home can mean

In shadowed stillness
I glide into myself
A sigh escapes
I know peace.

Contents

Preface

Near my childhood home, there was a cow pasture where I spent hours playing. A deeply rutted dirt track crossed the pasture; it emerged from the woods and snaked its way through the grass and continued on into the next pasture. The track meandered its way through one field after another as far as I could see, heading west.

My older brother told me that the dirt track had been part of the Santa Fe Trail and I half believed him. I wanted to believe that something as romantic as the famous Santa Fe Trail passed through my life. I would sit high in my favorite tree on the edge of the pasture and try to imagine who might have walked that trail and where they had been heading. I pictured myself taking such a journey someday. That rutted dirt track represented the ultimate journey to me; to put aside everything you know and venture out into wild uncharted territory with only a vague notion of where you would end up.

This book of essays is about my own journey years later and miles away from that rutted dirt track. It grew out of journals I kept during the seven years that I lived on three acres of grassland and woods in northeastern Kansas. This writing is my first foray into wild uncharted territory. Instead of exploring rivers and deserts and crossing mountains, I explore three small acres and my own inner landscape.

Like the travelers before me, I find both joy and sorrow on the trail. There are times when I want nothing better than to end my journey, to run away and hide from what my pen has discovered. Yet the trail keeps calling me back, whispering of new sights and adventures just over the next hill.

I hope you enjoy this travelogue of mine.

Beginning

Found

I remember when I first saw the land that would become my nest. My husband and I had searched for months and finally found a house on 3 acres not far from the city. It was called Morning Deer—a poetic name that I liked immediately.

My husband first took me out to see the place in early October 1994. I got out of the car that day and instantly felt like I was home. Something in the bend of the light through the trees—or maybe it was the surface of the pond water rippling in the breeze. Whatever it was, something told me I was home, that this place was where I was meant to live. The house was hideous; a mix of bad construction and 1970's carpet and paint. My husband tried to point out its many flaws to me, but I would not be dissuaded.

> *Journal excerpt: It's been a wild month. We found a house in the country on three wooded acres with a big pond—a gorgeous, wonderful spot. We put our house in KC on the market and sold it in 4 days! I guess we're moving to the country in a month. I still can't quite believe it. The new house is in a spot like I have dreamed of living in. And now we will live there. I am blessed.*

To anyone else this little plot of land probably looks like a dull Kansas hillside: A grass covered hill, a mossy pond, a grove of tangled, old Osage Orange trees, and a small meadow full of weeds. But the land called to me like an old friend with a delectable secret to share. I was meant to live here even if it was a totally illogical purchase. With lots of paint and a little remodeling, we made the house barely livable. My husband, 2-year old son and I moved in before Christmas.

Quiet

When I moved to this hilltop, I had no idea how many lessons I would learn here. Looking back, I notice now how much the place reminds me of the spot where I grew up—the trees and the water, the angle of the early morning sun through the dining room windows, the open meadow. And the silence, always the silence.

When friends come out to visit, the first thing they say is "It's so quiet!" It is true—I never realized how noisy the suburbs are until I moved here. The constant hum of city traffic is noticeably absent. You hear the soft wind in the leaves. A lawn mower running a mile away seems outrageously loud. The silence of this place envelops my body like a warm glove.

> *Journal excerpt: I am in a new space. Quiet mist wraps the land. Not a breath seems to stir. My baby is breathing safe in dreamland. Refrigerator hum fills the room with a monotonous drone. Cats pace the floor looking for an open lap. White winter sky stretches as far as my gaze can follow. Home is a warm place to be today.*

I have always been a quiet person. As a child my favorite spot was high up in a tree with only the sun and wind for company. But I was taught that being quiet and soft-spoken was a bad trait—a liability. My naturally boisterous mother worried that my lack of chatter signaled a problem. In school I was pushed to speak up, speak out if I wanted an A. As an adult, my boss complained that I was too soft-spoken, too quiet—not forceful enough to be taken seriously.

Out in the world, I am expected to speak up and be forceful if I want to succeed. But here amongst the trees, my soft and quiet nature fits right in. I seem to flow in the natural silence. Here on this land I belong.

Journey

I leave the office as the sun is inching close to the horizon. It was a typical day at the office; I attended 5 meetings and spoke with 50-60 people, responded to at least that many voice-mail and e-mail messages and prepared a slide presentation on the growth of PC use throughout the organization. I also got very close to moving enough papers to actually see the bottom of my in-basket. Was I productive? I felt productive at the time. I 'did' a lot of stuff. Now I am finished for the day and ready to journey home.

I get in my car and hurry up and wait. It takes me 10 minutes to traverse the 5 blocks to the highway entrance ramp. Ahh, the joys of rush hour in the city. The radio blares drive-time commercials designed to convince me to part with some money. I turn the radio off and hear silence for the first time in hours. The quiet feels so good to my tired brain. I did not even realize how frazzled I was until I found a quiet space.

Traffic is a little heavy as I circle the edge of the suburbs. I push my way impatiently through hundreds of vehicles heading home. Finally I turn south and head out of the city sprawl. Traffic thins out and I put my car on auto-pilot. I am half-way home.

I have been mentally chewing on my day, but as the traffic clears, my mind also starts to clear. The sky seems huge out here where the cows outnumber the people. The sky is an ever-changing canvas filled with color and form. From huge ominous gray-green thunderheads towering over me to wisps of high white cirrus cloud edged orange by the setting sun. As usual, the sky puts on a show for my drive home. I find myself daydreaming about magical cloud islands floating in the sky. My work tensions slowly melt away.

My favorite drives are actually when the sky is hidden from view. I love driving home in fog. It may be dangerous, but I find it fascinating to drive through fog. Some odd formation of land and creek-beds causes fog to hug the landscape close to my home on many spring and fall evenings. When I drive into the mist, it is almost as if I disappear. Poof! The trees and grass and road are gone, leaving a silvery nothingness behind. White shrouded objects appear suddenly next to the road, and then are gone in a flash. The world becomes just the present moment; no future in sight, no past to revisit, just now.

The last few miles to my house are on gravel road. No more well maintained asphalt roads out here. Gravel separates the men from the boys in the country. Gravel roads are pocked and rutted. They are slick when it rains or snows and blanket the car in dust when it is dry. Everything on the edge of a gravel road is coated in fine gray powder. You can tell someone lives out here by the coating of gray dust on his or her car. There is one good thing about gravel—it keeps the tourist traffic to a minimum.

I am almost home now. Pick up the mail and turn the car down the long drive. The hill is still here. My busy day and my to do list are now completely forgotten.

My car is a dusty mess, the grass needs mowing, and the house trim is peeling. None of that really matters. What I focus on is the sky above me. It is a deep pink with orange marshmallow highlights.

I go to the back patio and sit on the swing and breathe in the silence. Here on the hill, it feels fine to just sit and be. No action required—no phone call, no memo, no meeting. Just be.

Country

My son is named after a famous English king. His name means estate ruler in Olde English. Little did his father and I know how appropriate that name would turn out to be. At the ripe old age of 4, he is absolutely certain that this world is his kingdom—he is King of this hill.

My favorite photo of the "King" was taken in the front yard here on the hill when he was 3 years old. The grass is high, up past his knees. He is dressed in a striped T-shirt and long blue shorts. He has on his grubby black rubber boots and they are caked with mud. His little knobby knees jut out in the space between his boots and shorts. He is just a skinny little boy, but he is holding a giant stick as though he is a courageous knight going into battle with his lance. He seems transformed into a knight in search of imaginary dragons.

My son adores living in the country. He says authoritatively in his little voice that he is a "country boy", NOT a city boy. He loves to put on his boots and just hang out by his fort outside. I see him out there digging in mounds of dirt, turning over rocks in search of bugs, and fighting imaginary beasts with his huge lance. His idea of heaven is a hike down to the little stream below the pond dam.

I can relate to my "country boy". I absolutely loved being outside when I was young. I had a favorite tree that I spent hours sitting in, daydreaming away entire summer afternoons. It was cool and quiet, no brothers or sister would bother me when I was perched up in my tree overlooking the pasture.

I remember wading in the muddy creek behind my childhood home. It was rocky on the bottom with muddy banks and it ended in a little pool. Every little rock ripple was a raging waterfall in my young mind. I can still feel the cold rocks bruising my soles as I waded barefoot down the middle of the fast moving water. I loved the feel of the mud oozing up between my toes as I climbed the bank.

Kid heaven! I built stick dams with the neighbor boys and floated leaf boats toward Mexico. I can almost feel the hot sun on my back as I bend down to watch a water bug ballet up close. Oh, to be back there now!

My best memories of childhood happened outside in the water and the woods. And now I can give my son the gift of just hanging out with Mother Nature. I think that may be the best I have to offer him. Playing in nature feels like touching the essence of God to me. My son already seems to understand how sacred a natural space can be. I am happy to help him learn that.

I think I first experienced God playing in the trees and the water around my childhood home. I did not call it God then. And it took losing it to realize how important it was to me. I lost track of my spiritual side for years. I professed I was an atheist and I was quite content living in the tidy suburbs.

But a few years ago, I began to dream of wild open spaces where the lawns weren't manicured and the bushes were not trimmed to perfect symmetry. And at the same time, I began to meditate and search for a God that fit for me.

Is it just coincidence that my yearning for wild spaces popped up at the same time I began searching for God? No, a part of me always held onto the feeling I had when I played in the woods as a child. I remember that blissful feeling of being connected to all around me; the utter joy and contentment as I played with God, in God.

I think my God has lived outside amongst the trees ever since I first sat in a wind-blown tree on the edge of a cow pasture and stared at sunlight falling through the leaves. That sunlit tree was more beautiful than any man-made cathedral window I have ever seen.

And now my son is King of this windblown and wild sacred hill. I have come full circle. This is truly home.

Magic

Dance

There is a grove of gnarled old Osage Orange trees on my back hill. The Latin name for the Osage Orange tree is Maclura Pomifera, but I like its nickname better: Hedge. The Hedge tree is a native Midwest tree and a member of the Mulberry family. It got its nickname because early settlers used it to create hedges and windbreaks along the fence lines all over the prairie.

A Hedge tree is not something most suburban gardeners prize. These are not glamorous trees like Oaks or Maples or ornamental Weeping Cherry trees. For one thing the female Hedge trees create large fruit balls every summer. Hedge fruit balls are big grapefruit-sized orbs with a rough yellow-green exterior and a sticky seed-filled interior. According to <u>Wyman's Garden Encyclopedia</u>, there is *nothing* ornamental about Hedge fruit. I must agree.

In the fall when the Hedge balls ripen and fall, it can be dangerous to stand under our hedge trees. And the balls make quite a mess when they come crashing to the ground. Hedge trees also drop their leaves early in the fall and are one of the last trees to leaf out in the spring. This means the trees are bare for months. All in all, Hedge trees are considered "trash trees" by most gardeners.

But I have grown to love these trees. They may not be a good fit in the suburbs, but out here on this hilltop, they fit perfectly. Kind of like me, I guess.

I love their toughness; these trees do not blow down in a stiff breeze. Hedge wood is rock hard. The wood is so hard that few insects will touch it. The early settlers on the prairie prized hedge wood for use as fence posts and building joists because it is tough as nails and resists rot for decades.

Hedge trees also live a long, long time. I like that kind of tenacity. And I like the way their tree limbs twist and turn and tangle together. There is no symmetry, no obvious pattern in the arrangement of branches on a Hedge tree. Each branch seems to have a mind of its own as it grows toward the sky. They are total nonconformists—I seem to like that in my trees, and my friends.

The Hedge trees on my hill look a little mean and unfriendly at first glance. Their bark is rough and each limb is riddled with short spiky thorns. But hidden beneath the rough exterior of a Hedge tree is a deep burnished orange heart. Orange is a power color—very fitting for such a powerful tree. When I burn Hedge wood on cold nights, the wood burns fiery hot for hour after hour. The heart of a Hedge tree can be counted on to burn strong and bright when put to the test.

Maybe that's the lesson I have learned from these Hedge trees; no matter how rough and prickly the exterior, there is always a beautiful prize waiting to be found just beneath the surface if only I take the time to look. This is true of trees and people and every other living thing. The Universe does not waste energy. Every person, every plant, every animal has some gift to offer—even "trash" trees.

In the Wizard of OZ, Dorothy and the scarecrow pass through an enchanted forest where the trees move and talk. The magical trees have gnome-like faces etched into their trunks and their voices are low and gruff. When the trees get angry, they throw their fruit at Dorothy and the scarecrow. I remember being fascinated by those trees when I watched the Wizard of OZ as a young girl. I wished for trees like that in my own back yard—magical talking trees with quirky personalities and care-worn faces.

And now I look around this Kansas hilltop and see my enchanted forest come to life. Like wizened old sages, the Hedge grove has guarded this hilltop for more than 50 years. And when the wind blows, the trees bow gracefully and dance. They creak and groan with age and share all of the secrets of this magical hilltop with me.

Darkness

If I go outside on a cloudless night and look up from this hilltop, I fall into a million stars. The sky seems endless. It is so dark out here away from the lights of the city. I used to be afraid of the dark as a child. But now I go outside and the sky is like a twinkling quilt that blankets me and keeps me safe and warm.

To the north of my hill the night sky is lit year-round with a yellowish surreal glow. It is the lights of the city spilling out into the darkness. When I drive home from the city at night, I love leaving those lights behind. Mile by mile, the road grows darker and quieter. The suburbs thin out and then vanish into dark and silent farmland.

The transition from light to dark, from city noise to natural quiet calms me and slows down my inner rhythm. I am like a newborn baby who will stop crying and grow calm if just moved to a dark and quiet space. A respite from the light and noise of the city is all I need to calm myself.

Many people fear darkness. And silence. They blanket their houses in lights and make the radio or TV a constant companion to ward off their fear. I wonder how many people walk around in a constant state of overload from the barrage of light and noise? Maybe that is why some city dwellers can be so cranky and unfriendly; like a newborn baby they just need to be gently rocked in a quiet, dark room for awhile.

My mom grew up without electricity. She remembers evenings filled with the flickering light from gas lanterns. There was no radio and no TV. When it got dark, she went to bed and talked and snuggled with her sister. Today we turn on the lights and stay up late watching TV or surfing the Web. We ignore the rhythms of the sun and stay up half the night. And then wonder why we can't slow our minds down enough to sleep! Sometimes I think all these modern conveniences make it harder to create a peaceful and happy life.

I am struck by the thought that plants require time in the dark to grow. I remember my old botany professor detailing the intricacies of the "dark phase" during photosynthesis—a time when magical mysterious chemical reactions somehow transform sunlight into leaf and bark and flower. Humans also grow in the dark. Our cells repair themselves and divide at night while we are in deepest sleep. Darkness is a little understood space where true miracles occur.

I go outside in the fading light of dusk and watch the stars appear to my eyes one by one. As the sky turns velvet black in the spaces between each star, I remember what darkness is for.

My body has a genetic memory of ancient nights spent huddled in the safety of my tribe near the dying embers of a communal fire. Deep in my flesh I know that darkness is made for slowing down and stopping the activities of the day. Darkness is a time for reconnecting and snuggling close to my family. And darkness is for quiet sleepy dreams that wash my turbulent mind clean.

I wonder how much magic I miss when I avoid the dark and quiet spaces in life?

Solstice

It is the first day of summer. Today is officially the Summer solstice—the longest day of the year. And a full moon hung low in the sky last night. The day seems positively pregnant with possibility. Anything can happen.

I walk the long expanse of mown grass, feeling blades tickle my toes and ankles. Looking up, I see stark white billowing thunderheads to the east and north. Blue sky is directly above me. Summer is glorious on this hill.

I reach the dock and look out across the pond. The water is dead still, an unrippled clear green pool that sings to me. As I prepare to dive into the water, I notice hundreds of tiny raindrops suddenly hitting the surface of the pond, sending little ripples in all directions. One little wisp of a cloud is blessing me with teardrops for mother earth. On this day of summer solstice, the sunlit raindrops seem like a special gift just for me.

The entire weekend has been a gift. I attended a healing workshop yesterday with an energetic healer from Sedona. He was a strange intense man who filled the room with soft energy. It was a day of flowing energy and incredible emotional release. It felt like another nexus point in my journey within myself. And now the raindrops bless me with liquid coolness.

I dive into the water, feel it part and caress my skin. I send big ripples across the pond in all directions and think about how I will do that in the world. Exactly how is still veiled and unclear, yet I know it will be.

The water breaks around me as I dive under the surface. I am enclosed in a cocoon of warm, safe wetness. I move slowly through the cloudy green light and feel liquid joy surround me. Listening to silence, I swim stroke after stroke. Just one more, then another and another until I am forced to pull myself to the surface and gasp for air.

I float on my back, barely moving, and gaze up into a brilliant blue sky edged in marshmallow clouds reflecting the colors of the setting sun. Day is done and I am at peace.

Later, at twilight, I sit and watch fireflies dance beneath the tree canopy. They seem drawn to shine their light in the darkest places. And in doing so, they are all the more radiant. I think of the dark places in my life and wonder how I can bring light to them. All in good time.

Mother God danced in me today, a liquid green stillness. And my soul remembered who I am.

Death

I look out the patio door and see that a cloud has descended on top of the pond. For the second time this week, the perfect mix of temperature, humidity and windless air has caused the back hill and pond to recede into a silvery mist. I throw on my clothes, in a hurry to take a walk in the clouds.

As I wash my hands in the bathroom, a small, leggy brown spider swirls toward the drain. At first I am sure that I have killed it, and I guiltily try to wash it away down the drain and out of sight. Once, twice, three times I try to wash my cardinal sin away. On the third try, I detect a leg flicker. Fishing the spider out of the sink, it springs instantly back to life. Stretching and shaking its legs free of entanglement, the spider quickly arises as if it is Lazarus returning from the dead. My heart smiles at the wonder of a spider with nine lives.

The mist has started to clear as I finally head down the back hill. The sun is just cresting over the dam ridge and the cloud swirls around me as it slowly evaporates. The hill is studded with the webs of hundreds of funnel spiders. Funnel-shaped webs of all sizes cling to the grass, evidence of the life and death hunt that plays out every night in the shadowy dark on this hill.

Walking around the north edge of the pond, I am lost in thought. Suddenly, a ray of sun catches the edge of a huge bulls-eye shaped web directly in front of me. This web covers half the path at eye level and is constructed with perfect symmetry. There is no way for me to pass without tearing it and I notice that its owner is still in residence. I take this as a sign to turn around. As I turn to go, I catch sight of the frantic beating of small wings out of the corner of my eye.

A white butterfly with one orange and one black spot at the base of each wing is caught in a ragged web by the side of the path. Beating its wings over and over, it cannot escape the sticky web. As I pause to look, a tiny spider, russet colored save the white triangle on its abdomen, climbs onto the back of the winged creature. I watch in paralyzed horror as the tiny spider rides the struggling butterfly like a bronco rider and bites it again and again. After many long seconds, the butterfly hangs motionless in the web. When movement stops, the spider deftly cuts two threads and rappels down beneath the dying butterfly. In a matter of seconds, the tiny spider entombs the butterfly in silken thread and moves on to repair the web.

I watch and contemplate all the struggle and pain and death that lie just below the surface of the natural world; gorgeous webs ensnaring a spider's next meal; soaring flycatchers snatching mayflies from the air; robins pecking apart wriggling earthworms and swallowing them piece by piece. No matter how much I wish for a life filled with only beauty and joy, the opposite qualities must be present. Yin and Yang, light and dark, good and evil; the duality of nature surrounds me.

I find a sodden young robin in the grass as I head back up the hill. Thinking it might still be alive, I reach down to move it up into the tree. Just before I touch it, I realize that its eye socket is empty. Then I see a roly-poly crawling slowly over the robin's wet back. I pull back in revulsion. I am saddened by this image of death, yet somehow joyful that life swirls on relentlessly in the grass all around it. This robin may now be worm food, but I am heartened by the memory of Lazurus the spider, alive and well in my bathroom.

I move on up the long hill, pondering a morning filled with death and rebirth.

Butterfly

I lie in the hammock, slowly gliding and thinking about my day. A list of would have, should have, could have is rapidly lengthening in my mind. Suddenly, my glance is pulled to the tree in front of me. The leaves seem to be fluttering in the dead calm afternoon air. I realize after a second and third glance that it is not leaves fluttering but rather butterflies—hundreds of butterflies.

The tree appears to be under butterfly attack. Countless small tan butterflies flit from branch to branch. There are long brown seedpods hanging from the locust tree and I wonder if that is the attraction. The tree has long since flowered so there is no obvious nectar source.

As I watch the tree 'dance', the reason for the deluge of butterflies fades in importance. What is important is the effect—the tree seems to have grown wings and a mind of its own. Tree becomes animal and is magically transformed before my eyes.

And the shock of seeing a tree sprout wings pulls me utterly and completely into the present. For a few moments in time, I am totally aware of what is going on around me and in me. No more ruminating over the past or planning my future, I am planted firmly in that rocking hammock enjoying one moment in time, joyful at the sight of a tree that flies.

Later as I sit in the shade on the deck, the butterflies return. I watch in amazement as hundreds of tiny dive-bombers storm the bread and grapes on the shelf feeder. One alights on my arm and gives me angel kisses that tickle my flesh.

Butterfly lives are very short in human terms, but they seem to live life to the hilt while they are here. Fly, find food and mate—it sounds pretty fantastic to me—much more appealing right now than my to-do list of paying bills and returning phone calls.

The next morning as I hurriedly back the car out of the garage, late as usual, a cloud of butterflies engulfs the car. I gasp in awe and pause to watch the fluttering cloud of wings. My son looks up from his book to ask, "Why are butterflies all over the car, Mom?" Smiling, I reply, "I don't know…but aren't they wonderful?" The rest of my morning seems blessed by angels. It is the little serendipitous moments that make my life magical.

Growth

Plant

This gardener has met her match. I used to have a big garden back in the suburbs, filled with all kinds of flowers and vegetables. I was blessed with a green thumb—I could grow pretty much anything I set my mind to. But my thumb seems to have rusted or something. Here in the country surrounded by trees and wild grasses and wildflowers, I am a gardening failure.

I blame the weather. I seemed to have moved into an area that is bypassed by every other rainstorm. I have nicknamed this place the "banana belt". I can drive out of the city in a blinding rainstorm, but when I get within a few miles of my hill, the rain stops and it is bone dry. So, that's my excuse—not enough rain.

But every spring I still get the planting urge. And I fantasize that maybe this year will be different. I pour through seed catalogs and select just the right seeds. This year I even trucked in rich black river-bottom dirt with the hope of ending my gardening jinx. No such luck. Here is my pathetic vegetable harvest for the year: a handful of scrawny, pale tomatoes, one small pot of green beans, 6 green onions and 1 cup of jalapeno peppers. The corn died, rabbits ate my lettuce, and deer ate most of my green beans. My pumpkins never even tried to set fruit. And tulips appear to be some kind of delicacy for deer.

Uncle! I think my gardening days are over. I still carry around a gorgeous image of the perfect vegetable garden in my mind. This fantasy garden is a tangle of lush green plants that hang heavy with fruit. I look out at my sun scorched garden patch—the only thing lush and green are the weeds. I am finding it hard to let go of my attachment to homegrown vegetables. No more juicy tomatoes right off the vine. No more sweet corn from my own patch. My mouth waters just thinking of what I will miss.

I have found one solace for my bruised gardener's ego: prairie wildflowers grow without any tending here. I can just toss the seed out and up they will spring. And a few months later, they bloom for weeks in every color of the rainbow.

Maybe this land is just persnickety. I guess only tough and hardy native souls need apply for a spot on this hilltop. I am just relieved that this hill has allowed me to plant myself here and grow. Luckily I don't need much water.

Naked

I lost my smile for awhile this morning. I was feeling sad and lonely, so I went outside and dug in the dirt. I planted shrub roses—one of the few plants tough enough to share this hill with me. I frowned and I dug and I searched for a little peace. By the time I was finished I felt better but my hands were shredded. I should have worn gloves but I prefer naked hands when I dig in the dirt.

There is something very primal about sinking my fingers down into the ground and immersing myself in Mother Earth. My style of gardening demands naked, vulnerable hands. What that means is my hands get cut and scraped up. But I also have the amazing experience of sinking wrist deep into cool moist earth. I get to play in powdery topsoil and slick clay like a child in a sandbox. I enjoy the feel of wriggling earthworms and hairy root balls between my fingers.

Gardening is a tactile and sensual pleasure without gloves. And it is also dangerous. Digging around in the dirt with naked hands is very vulnerable and probably a little crazy. After a morning of "naked" gardening my hands look like I went to war and lost. A sensible person would wear gloves. I am supposed to be a sensible person. I get paid a lot of money to be a very logical and sensible computer systems manager. But there is also a totally illogical and emotional side to life that I will never get to experience if I am sensible and logical all the time. So, I live on the edge and garden without gloves.

Life is a lot like gardening. I can put on a glove and cover up my soft vulnerable flesh. I can present an impervious sensible exterior to the world and act like I am tough and invulnerable. Or I can leave myself exposed and show my heart and my soft emotional core to the world. The second option is rife with danger. Someone could take advantage of me, of my softness. They could use me or hurt me badly. That is a very scary possibility. But I cannot stomach the alternative. The thought of living hidden behind a tough shell is not appealing to me.

My son meets the world with soft eyes and an open heart. He does not hold back and wait to see if it is completely safe to smile or to reach out and love someone.

He reminds me what it looks like to be utterly alive and open to everything life offers. I wonder what the world could be like if adults were able to be that open.

Humans are meant to be soft and caring and vulnerable. Those are some of our best qualities. We are meant to be open and soft enough to enjoy intimacy with our family, with our friends and neighbors, with the natural world. The best moments of my life are when I risk it all and share my true naked self with the world.

Cultivate

Now that I have my dream castle on a hill, I am wondering what my next step is. The word that comes to me when I meditate on my future is "cultivate". But cultivate what? Gardening has not exactly been a resounding success for me lately. Maybe cultivate refers to something else, something not quite so literal. Perhaps I should have another baby? Write a book? What exactly should I cultivate?

Yesterday's all-day meeting at work was intense and exhausting. I feel like parts of this job are so UN-me. It's like trying to force myself into a shape that doesn't quite fit. To fit the mold I have cut off pieces of myself. It horrifies me that I might permanently lop off the writer piece of me trying to fit some corporate mold.

So, can I break the mold? Or find a new job, a new mold? What is next for me? I am afraid I have been taking care of everyone but myself. I focus on what my family needs at home. And what my boss and my staff want at work. Maybe I should put myself back into the equation. I did when I insisted on buying this hilltop. Can I keep standing up for what I want? *What exactly do I want and need?*

At work I look around and find I have been cultivating my boss's garden, her dream of what our department should be like. And at home I have been cultivating my husband's dream patch. It is high time I cultivated my own patch of earth. I am not certain that I know how to do that.

I just had the flash of an image: I am working in the middle of a garden that is just starting to bloom. But I look over the fence and see my own little garden patch. My patch is sad and pitiful, neglected and almost choked out by weeds. I get up and go to my garden and dig in.

Hmmm. That is exactly what I have been doing with my pen—digging in and cultivating myself. Maybe my green thumb has been transformed into a writing pen. That's all well and good, but I still miss growing tomatoes.

Cleanse

Tiny grasshoppers jump and buzz with every step as I walk around the pond. The ground at my feet is dry and cracked, aching for a long soaking shower. Summer seems to have arrived even though it is only the middle of May. The pond is in full bloom. I sit on the dock and peer down into water filled with billowy green algae clouds. The green clouds waft by in slow motion, in perfect synchrony with the clouds high overhead. I watch the clouds dance and smile in wonder.

An hour later, I look up from my writing chair and discover the sky darkening outside the window to the south. It is a deep ominous blue, the shade that precedes thunderstorms on the plains. Then twisted yellow lightning bolts etch the sky beyond the treetops. The smell of rain comes on a sudden breeze. The dry cracked earth by the pond will get its wish now...

It was a gully washer of a storm. Wind, hail and rain ripped from the sky and flashes from lightning to the south turned darkest night into a surreal yellow-green dusk. I sat huddled in my basement, corralled by tornado warnings, and watched in awe as Mother Nature flexed her muscles.

This morning a brand new world greets me on my walk. Not a single grasshopper is in sight or earshot. I wonder where grasshoppers disappear to when it rains? A brown snake lies curled next to the path in the middle of the dam. The snake looks stunned and lethargic and I wonder if his home was washed away in last night's deluge.

Deep, lush moist green is everywhere. New shoots of grass are sprouting up in every nook and cranny. What was dry, parched soil is now a spongy, waterlogged blooming marsh. The drainage gully from the meadow into the pond is noticeably enlarged and now threatens the very existence of my favorite path. The tired heat of yesterday is nowhere to be found.

Mother Nature has the right idea, having the rain and hail and wind sweep through the land. A gully washer of a storm is exactly what the parched earth needed to recover and bloom anew. I am reminded of a time a few weeks ago when I felt dry and parched tired of life, tired of myself. I became frenetic, busily avoiding my feelings for days. But when I finally stopped trying to maintain control, when I let go and just sat with myself, I found myself wracked with sobs. I was soon awash in pain and sorrow.

At first I did not even know what my sadness was about. But as I cried, I remembered a hurtful rejection several days earlier. I had told myself at the time that I was fine; I would not let the rebuff bother me. I ended up ruining more than a few days trying to avoid feeling sad. And just like the thunderstorm last night, when I finally let it rip, my inner storm soon passed. I woke up the next morning and I felt lush and alive again.

Whether it is a rainstorm or tears, nothing can match the cleansing effect of a good gully washer.

Faith

I was writing in a journal off and on for several years before I moved to this hill-top. But in this new place, my writing has moved to center stage. I feel compelled to explore this hill and its effect on me. I find myself pouring hours into walking the land and then writing about it. My high-powered computer career has become secondary. For years I have been buried in the intricacies of making computers work. Now I find myself pulled in a new direction. Exploring me in this new place is what sings to my soul now.

Yet in the writing is a tension. I am both attracted and repelled by this process of peeling back layers and uncovering what lies beneath. Some days I can not put my pen down. Others I can not will myself to pick it up and start.

> *Journal excerpt: Tired, tired. I want sleep, but I need to write—it's my only chance. That's not really true, though. I watched TV for 1 1/2 hours when I could have been writing. I could write for an hour or two each day. Just do it. On my deathbed will I regret missing a TV show?*

> *What does it mean when I say I want to write, yet I never have time? No, I never make time—there is time for writing but I waste it watching the boob tube and other trivialities.*

The parts of me I am beginning to uncover are not always so wonderful. And there are a million easy distractions that I can use to avoid writing. I stall and putter around the house and ignore my writing chair. And I grow cranky and chaotic inside. But when I do finally talk myself into sitting down to write, my chaos finds order and I grow calm and quiet within.

I get up and go into the kitchen, looking for a distraction—something to take me away from my pen and pad. As I daydream and look out my window, I spy yellow edged leaves. The hedge trees on the back hill are turning. And the sumac—I remember the sumac was a mix of red and green on the edge of the meadow yesterday. Autumn is here. It seems only yesterday it was a sticky 99 degrees in the shade and now autumn has arrived.

I hear honking and look beyond the hedge grove. The geese that inhabit the pond are in chaos. They young ones are flying crazily, almost drunkenly, up and down the length of the pond. They are disturbed, excited—something is up. Is it time to head south? Are southern waters calling to them? I do not hear the call, but I see their frenzy as they circle. Their journey is at hand.

I wonder where these geese fly off to every year. Do they winter in Mexico, soaking up the warm sun while I shiver in the Kansas prairie wind? Or do they prefer Christmas at the Alamo? Perhaps they stop off in Oklahoma for a visit to reservation lands. Wherever they end up, is there someone there to watch and analyze their every interaction?

I watch them circle and honk. It must be scary for the young geese to feel the urge to leave and not know where they will end up. Kind of like writing. Something inside you says it is time to make the journey. You are frightened and excited all at once. You grow agitated and circle around and around, trying to find the courage to begin. Finally you take a deep breath and start. The next thing you know you look up and you are miles from where you started. And once you get there, you cannot remember quite how you managed to do it.

Traversing new territory, whether by wing or by pen, must be done on faith. Take a deep breath and start.

If those young geese can find the courage, then so can I. I head back to my pen and pad. I begin again, one stroke at a time with only my faith to guide me.

Birth

I am here, right here
I feel your pulse dance within
Joy dissolves my fear.

Fog shrouds my hill this morning. And my mind. I head out for a long walk in the mist to clear away my mental cobwebs. The winter air is surprisingly warm. The smell just hints at spring, although I know this is illusion. This is the heart of winter and spring is weeks away.

The trees are suspended in cloud. My normal world has been transformed into something mysterious and still. It is odd how just a touch of mist in the air can shift my perception of this place, this space I know so well. This hill so familiar to me appears shockingly new today. I look around with new eyes.

The pond is molasses; slowly undulating liquid solid. It is as though the water cannot decide whether to stand silent or let go and flow. I stand next to the dock and watch this molasses dance. I also cannot decide whether to stand silent and watch or move.

I finally break free of the water's dance and walk around the pond path. I spy a curve of creek through the bare tree limbs. An icy white S delineates the space where creek meets land. It reminds me of smoke frozen in time waiting for the slightest breeze to free it. This world sits patiently and waits.

A quiet trickle of water music fills my ears. Water is moving, flowing somewhere close that I cannot quite see. This land looks dead and barren, yet the water flows. I sense the slow steady heartbeat of Mother Earth in that quiet trickle. Just below the surface life waits. The earth is resting, growing, and gathering strength. Soon new growth will burst forth here.

And within me as well. I carry new life in my belly, my womb. I carry new life. Like a mantra, that thought consumes me today. I carry new life. What I already knew in my bones was confirmed by a test yesterday. I carry new life. I feel a new energy stirring, quickening within me; just below my surface. And already I am changed. I have 9 months of waiting, watching, growing and changing as I help this new life surface in the world. Nine months of wonder before I see this new being with my eyes.

A new child is joining my family. I am joyful, excited, scared and humbled. Within me is a new child—so much responsibility. And so much joy. Thank you God for this blessing.

Peace

Flow

I listen to a freight train on the other side of the ridge as it rumbles south. I stop writing for a moment and wonder where the train is headed.

The house grows quiet now and the train whistle echoes in my ears. I am lulled by soft breathing over the monitor on my nightstand. My perpetual motion machine son is finally at rest. I sit and take stock of the day, the weekend, my life. It was a pleasant weekend full of cleaning and errands and play; restful and calm days with this incredible child I am raising.

I caught myself rushing him today when it was not necessary. A little ah ha for me about pushing and not giving him space to just be himself. Sometimes I act like that freight train with a rigid schedule to keep. Do I want to teach my child to be a freight train hurrying to his destination, or a rocky stream meandering slowly through a sunlit meadow? I gaze at my son sprawled over his bed in sleep and see a stream.

I am drawn to tree shadows on the water. It is as though water holds the key to my day. Will it be smooth and calm, or endless wind and waves?

I fight against the current of my life at times. Other times I float serenely in the flow, not knowing or caring where it leads. My son knows a lot about going with the flow and finding peace, if only I will watch him and let him teach me.

Oscillations

The trees are still today and the morning air is heavy. July in the Midwest is not for wimps. I walk out of the house at mid-day and the heat hits me, taking my breath away with its force. Five minutes in the sun and my shirt is dripping. I am glistening with sweat and dreaming of just a hint of a spring breeze.

The dog days of summer are here. My favorite spot to play dead is in the hammock under the locust tree in the side yard. I lie supine, barely twitching a muscle and wish for a slave to fan me. Ice from my drink applied to the neck is like ecstasy. But when it quickly melts away, I am left wanting more.

Summer reminds me that anything good taken to extreme soon becomes oppressive and unwelcome. In the frigid, dark days of February, I fantasize of summer heat and my hammock. And as the spring turns to summer here, the sun is still welcome and comforting. Now with sun at the apex of its powers, I shrink from it and dream of cool, shady days when it does not shine at all.

The weather extremes of the Midwest push at my limits and remind me that moderation can be a good thing. I am not very good at moderation. It does not come naturally to me. I want to push at the boundaries and continually expand my life in all directions. Like a pendulum at the beginning of its swing, I sometimes swing wildly from one edge to another as I try to create the "perfect" life. And when I slow down and begin to slowly oscillate around midpoint, I quickly grow bored and begin looking around for another push toward the edge.

I want to learn how to enjoy the small oscillations of life that happen in the quiet moments—the subtle shifts in understanding, the tiny baby steps toward a far-away goal. I suspect that these little movements hold even more joy than the wild swings I am accustomed to.

If only I can remember to pause and be right where I am. Right here. Right Now. No big pendulum swing required. Just look around and BE here. That is where peace and joy live.

Fear

The grass on the back hill blows and bends in the icy wind. Tree branches creak and sway as though about to split and crash to the ground. Sun glints on rippling water—liquid light in motion. Leaves turn golden and fall to their death. The seasons roll on in a circular pattern, an endless cycle.

Today that cycle reminds me of a fight with my partner two days ago. Round and round covering the same ground. I am caught in a mire of missed connections and pain. Today I do not see the beauty of the natural cycle. There is only a negative repetition going on and on. I can scarcely remember the spring. I dream of escape.

In my mind's eye I am swimming in the cool green twilight. The depths surround and enclose. I feel the liquid touch of Mother Earth's tears. Muscles pumping, I propel myself toward the bottom, to the heart of the lake where the living beat is barely audible above the sound of my own fear.

I find myself in an up and down cycle of roller coaster emotions this week. Mount Everest highs and Pacific trench lows. I watch my pattern and worry at the extremes. I was never like this before, was I? It is like my Beast self is unleashed and roaming the subterranean passages of my soul, searching for a way out, for release. My Beast searches for flesh to chew and bones to crunch.

I will myself to let go, to stop trying to feel better. I am petrified that I will sink like a stone into this inky sadness, never to rise again. Yet part of me still hopes to rise through the water, breaking out at the surface and inhaling the sweet air all around. Inhaling what I need to plumb the depths of my shadows once more.

I blow out my breath and sink…

Grasp

I throw my pen down in disgust. Today I am not sad. Today I am angry.

I have been trying to finish an essay I started weeks ago, but the ending just will not come. The harder I try to force the ending, the further away it floats. It is like having a word on the tip of my tongue, but I can't quite access it. In total frustration I head down my favorite path for a walk.

I walk around the pond mentally berating myself for my inability to finish the essay. I scarcely see my surroundings. When I return to my land, I wander over to the dock, still deep in self-flagellation. I may not be much of a writer but I am an expert at self-flagellation.

As I sit on the dock, I keep hearing the sound of fish breaking the surface. Yet I cannot catch them in the act. It is just a sly, secretive flicker at the edge of water and sky that defies my eyes. The jumping fish are like seeds of thoughts in my subconscious that brush into my awareness and resist capture. The kind of thought that I am convinced would be a priceless gem if only it would surface long enough for me to catch its essence in the light.

Whatever the fish are up to, they now have my full attention. I scarcely breathe as I watch the water surface, waiting, waiting. But again and again I hear the sound of the water parting to my left or right, yet I see nothing but water ripples. I finally give up and just lounge on the dock, my eyes closed, soaking in the sun. As I get up to leave, a silvery fish jumps cleanly out of the water then dives out of view right in front of me. I could swear he was smiling at me.

I often catch myself wishing for what is not quite here. I push and grasp and try to force people and events to hurry up and do what I want. It rarely works out well.

Buddhist wisdom tells me if only I could learn to stop trying so hard; these flickering thoughts would become crystal clear to me. And then I would know true peace. The secrets of the Universe may lie in a silvery flicker, but I will never know until I let go of my need to grasp the secret, my need to control the outcome.

There's a Zen koan: Let go of my need to know and I will know all instantly. If I think about *that* too long, my head will explode…

Noise

I am engulfed in a host of new noises, natural noises. On this hilltop, the sound of summer is the drone of cicadas rising and falling in still hot afternoon air. The calls of birds evoke spring for me; "hello, look at me" songs fill the treetops in April and signal to me that spring has really arrived. Autumn is the crunch of dry leaves underfoot on the trail and the rustle of dying leaves overhead. And winter sounds like the relentless north wind, blowing mercilessly through the barren tree skeletons on the hill.

Every season here has a sound. And with every season there is a different feel in the air. Winter feels like deep, troubled sleep; Mother Earth is tossing and turning, looking for quiet repose. Then spring arrives feeling frenetic, busy—as though there is not nearly enough time to get everything done. Summer is sleepy and abundant; the earth is resting joyfully in her aliveness. Autumn comes and I feel a slowing of the pulse as the growing cycle slows down to a whisper.

Autumn is here now. I can feel it.

I lie in bed and listen to the sounds of night in these autumn woods; a cricket suddenly playing a violin solo in the silence. A solitary tree frog tentatively adding to the melody. The wind whispering through the leaves overhead. It is Zen music for my soul.

Cool crispness fills the autumn day. And now each cool and snuggly autumn night stretches before me silent and inviting. A comforter night filled with the scent and feel of my love's skin on mine. Synching up and exploring the nooks and crannies of each other as the crickets sing.

In the morning, there is mist in the valley. The second time this week. I look out of the kitchen window to discover that the pond no longer exists at the bottom of the hill. A silvery shroud has swallowed the pond whole, leaving a blank space at the bottom of the hillside. Not a breath of wind stirs. The morning mist feels sharp and cool in my throat, just as autumn air should feel. I can see my own breath ebb and flow as I stand on the deck straining to find the pond below.

My son chatters away in the dining room right behind me. As I peer out into the clouds, his chatter recedes and fades away. Life is still and utterly serene for a brief time. I find a little moment of peace in the midst of my morning chaos.

Wet

The peace and quiet of this hillside stimulates even more introspection than usual in me. And it stimulates memories of my childhood: I remember 'diving' in the bathtub as a child; holding my breath until it felt as though my chest would explode and splinter into a million pieces, I wanted to stay underwater longer and longer…forever if I could.

When I got a little older, I loved diving in the lake near my childhood home. I loved the shadowy green liquid world that muffled sound and touched my body so tenderly as I slid through it. I loved lake water the best; murky green wetness with yellow bars of light slanting down into the depths.

I am rediscovering the joys of 'bathtub diving'. I have been a shower person for years. Showers are so fast and functional; stand in the water, soap up, rinse off and jump out. From dirty to clean in a few moments time. But baths, ah, now baths are for soaking, for lounging, for dreaming. I seem to be more of a dreamer now that I am a country girl. I am definitely a bath person again. Time seems to moves slower on this hilltop. I find I have time to lounge in the tub and dream.

Here is my idea of the perfect bath: hot, hot water and a little vanilla bubble bath—just enough so the scent fills the tub. Then I sink in up to my ears. I like the water to fill my ears and muffle the sounds outside. I breathe in and out and watch my belly rise above the water with each in-breath and then sink beneath the surface like a little island being consumed by the ocean. I turn the water off and listen to my quiet breath. Bathtub diving is one of the most potent forms of meditation I have ever found.

I used to dream of being a fish, able to stay in liquid state forever. What a miracle it would be to have gills! It is the utter stillness that draws me back to water again and again.

The same stillness drew me to this house and pond amongst the trees. I sit in the silence here and I feel as though my soul is surrounded by shadowy green wetness. I am enfolded and caressed as I glide into the depths. Only now it is the depths of me that I plumb, not a muddy lake bottom. In this new space I need no gills—just myself and a few moments in the delicious silence.

Dharma

Money

The more I write, the more of myself I seem to uncover. I feel like an archeologist sifting through the remains of an Egyptian tomb. Only this is no ancient tomb I am sifting through, it is my soul.

I am discovering in this excavation that the writer and poet who had been hiding out for years inside of me do not really like corporate America. My *artiste* is clamoring for release from bondage. And the thrill of my high paying corporate job is gone. I used to get such a rush from being a competent, smart, well-respected computer network manager. Now I go to work and feel like Sisyphus, pushing the same boulder up the same hill day after day after day. There is no real progress, just a repeat of last week's problem in a new wrapper.

I sit in my office at work and fantasize about having more time to write. I calculate over and over how long my savings would last if I just quit. I can hardly believe this new me. I used to be so ambitious, so driven. I remember how I worked and pushed to get every promotion, to earn more money and more recognition. And now my heart just isn't in this job anymore. But it scares me half to death to consider leaving this job with its regular, predictable salary to write for a living. Ye Gods! How will I survive without a regular paycheck?

My parents grew up during the depression of the 1930's. They remember months of no money and very little food; they remember the embarrassment of having holes in their shoes and threadbare clothes to wear to school. They remember fathers that were laid off for months on end with no money coming in. A stable, good-paying job is Nirvana from my parents' perspective. And I absorbed their values early; keep the wolf from the door, find a good corporate job and work hard to advance. That is exactly what I have done.

I have my parents' values about money embedded in my every cell. And now when my soul is crying out "write, write, write!" my gut clenches in fear and I worry about how I will afford to buy food. Writing is not stable—no regular paycheck means certain disaster. Sooner or later my savings will run out and then I'll be left with just my pen and notebook while my financial house of straw blows down around me. That is the fear that comes up when I think of writing full-time.

But I look around me. I sit here writing and the floor is not made of straw, it is solid beneath my feet. And I feel so incredibly alive and connected to myself when I write. How can this be bad? This feeling of aliveness is worth a million dollars in the bank to me. I do not have a million dollars in the bank, but I do have savings. I could quit the corporate merry-go-round and just write for a year or two. Just write—it sounds so crazy.

Like my lungs and the breath that fills them, my pen and paper are a visceral part of me. I can lose my corporate job and still be fine. But if I lose my writing, I will lose the best and purest parts of me. And so I write.

Thaw

The sun is warm on my hair as I start down the slope that defines my backyard. Wet leaves underfoot make walking a thoughtful event. The sky is cloudless and pure blue; the tree branches are stark black in contrast. The pond sits smooth and silent, enclosed in an ice cocoon. Soon the waters will run free again, but for now the pond silently awaits thaw.

Today, I feel like that pond—cold and silent, wishing for a thaw.

I sent 3 poems to a journal, hoping against hope to become a published poet overnight. But today my poems were returned—thanks but no thanks. Gems now slightly tarnished returned to the fold. Amateur hour, no real writing here. I feel sad for my imperfect children rejected by the world. The words return bruised and battered, back to their mother for kisses and band-aid repair.

Questions rattle round my mind as I walk; what does a REAL writer look like? Act like? Smell like? How good is good enough? When can I stop polishing my gems and let them go? How will I know when I am THERE? Or does THERE ever become HERE? Is finished always just beyond the next horizon?

Not a soul is out. I have the pond and trees to myself. Yet the mushy ground beneath my feet is laden with signs of raccoon and deer and dog events. Many animals have passed this spot before me. And many writers have had to face the pain of rejection before me. I find little solace in reminding myself of all the now famous authors who were once rejected just like me.

I do not know where I am headed. But the sun is warm on my face and the land all around guides me on. I keep walking, one step at a time. Slowly, I feel my pain start to melt away. I am a work in progress; it is time pull out my pen and pad again.

A week later, I walk down the same path. A huge ice floe fills most of the pond. The ice is on the move, shifting with the water current that pulls it slowly south in the wind. Slowly, imperceptibly slowly it melts away. One molecule after another breaks free of its old bonds and joins the flow. In a day or two all that will be left of the icy structure is a cool memory.

I want to be like the ice, slowly melting my old personae away and joining the flow of life in a new direction. What current is pulling at me? Writing, always writing. Where is this flow going to lead? I feel my bonds shift and loosen as my soul expands into liquid state. Piece by piece I am writing a new me.

Change

I walk the pond path and chickadees announce my passing from their perch in the cedar grove. I crave a bit of time outside even though the wind still feels biting and cold. To escape the wind, I duck down the path that follows the creek. As I walk, I fantasize of digging in warm dirt and planting flowers even though I am surrounded by gray—gray tree trunks, gray sky, gray lifeless earth.

Not a hint of green can be found in the forest yet. Even the evergreens have a slight orange tint. The weeds under my boots are brown and lifeless. But wait—a hint of green! I spy the rounded edges of crocus leaves just beginning to erupt from the earth under the cedar trees.

Is it because the angle of the sun has shifted higher in the sky? Or is there some scent on the wind that my ancient reptilian brain picks up and responds to? Whatever the trigger, something deep and primal has been unleashed within me. Spring is close, very close—my body can sense it even before I spy those crocus leaves.

Today I want to dig in the dirt. Last night I had the irrational urge to scour my entire house clean and throw out half my belongings. Even my appetite has shifted. A week ago I wanted chili and bread. Today I crave green leafy salad and tomatoes. Somehow my tissues know that spring will be here very soon.

And I am not the only one. Even city dwellers feel the primal pull of spring. Two days ago, it was sunny all day and every other car I passed had its windows open even though the wind was icy cold. Forget the icy wind and the forecast for snow later this week; even normally sane adults go a bit mad when the primal pull of spring calls to them.

Ancient Germans worshipped Eostre in the spring. Eostre is a goddess of new growth, rebirth and springtime. She is also the basis for our modern day Easter egg celebrations. Her legend tells of a time when the spring thaw was late in coming and a little girl found a bird close to death in the forest. The girl called to

Eostre for help. A rainbow bridge appeared and Eostre came to the girl wrapped in a warm red robe that melted the snows. Spring arrived. But the bird was wounded beyond repair, so Eostre change him into a magical snow hare that brings rainbow colored eggs. And from that day forward, the return of the magical hare bearing eggs heralds spring. A bit of the Easter bunny and the Christian resurrection story all rolled into one legend.

But it is not the Easter Bunny that signals spring for me. It is the return of the geese to our pond that heralds spring's official arrival. They have not returned yet, but soon—soon they will be here. They are on their way back to the pond. I can feel it.

Two days later, I smell spring in the air. It is the smell of wet, living soil. Mother Earth is waking from her slumber. And the sky is suddenly blue today, no more flat winter gray. Overnight new buds bulge on every tree branch. I see green in the meadow. Tiny blades of grass push up through the dirt. A shift is afoot. The sun moves north, the earth heats. buds burst open and new life springs forth. Eostre is flirting with the earth like a wild and fertile young woman. Soon she will throw caution to the wind and embrace the hills in green.

I want to be like the coming of spring. I want to grow and push into a new way of being. I want to blossom with joy. I am struggling with leaving my job, my career of 11 years. Perhaps now is the time? I smell change in the air.

Bloom

My hard eyes broke and grew a rose
Whose one huge eye saw only you
Flowering in cosmos after cosmos
Laughing as we grew.
  —Rumi

I stomp down the pond path this morning, spewing mean and ugly thoughts. I am at odds with myself, questioning my self and my purpose. If I am meant to write, then why is it painfully hard this week? Again this morning I picked up my pen and nothing happened. My mind is totally blank. I search my thoughts and find nothing worth sharing. It is as though my creative faucet has stopped flowing. I throw down my pen and walk this familiar trail, hoping to find a few moment of peace.

What I find lining my path is flowers. Flowers are everywhere. The meadow overflows with so many blooms that the green of the grass is now just an accent. Tiny white daisies, pink clover, lilac liatris, yellow goldenrod. I am surrounded by small whispers of color and large flagrant displays. All sizes and shapes of flower are trumpeting life from every corner. I am drawn to these blooms—I stop and study all the shapes and hues and petal variations. No two flowers are exactly alike, yet all are similar.

Is that what human souls are like—infinite variations of shape and hue that reflect the divine in unique ways? I think of fractals; never repeating geometric patterns in nature. Their pattern is no pattern, yet they are made up of the same shapes underneath it all. The same essence is the foundation of everything.

I have a sudden sense of knowing that no matter what I choose to do with my gifts, no matter how much or how little writing I produce, I am always connected, always loved and supported by the Universe. I am a fractal among fellow fractals.

My feeling of connection fills me with peace. I head back up the hill to the house, back to my pen and paper with a new gleam in my eye. My creative juices are running again, thanks to a few delicious flowers.

Fling

I walk down the pond path this morning before the sun has crested over the tree line. The grass is high, to my waist in spots, with shiny maroon seed heads that look almost metallic. I look down and notice a star-like spider web next to the path. It is encrusted with jewels of dew that glisten in the early light. The web is engineered around a single tall stalk of prairie grass and is anchored on both sides with long strands disappearing into the brown grass blades below. I stop to examine the intricate star pattern.

Another web catches my eye and another and another. I am suddenly aware that spider webs are EVERYWHERE; perfect bulls-eyes, bowls, stars, triangles, pyramids, squares; every shape imaginable lines the bushes and grass on the edge of the meadow. All are shining with dew jewels in the early morning sunlight. The path is spider Mecca today and their handiwork takes my breath away.

Has there been a sudden surge in spider population or this is some last gasp spider fling before the first frost comes? Or have they been here for weeks and I was just too blind to notice?

My hike takes on a strange rhythm. I swing a long stick up and down in front of my face like a magician waving a magic wand—I want to break the webs before they tangle in my hair and clothes. I fall into a pattern; step, step, wave my wand, catch a web strand, break the strand, brush it aside and start over. Step, step, wave, catch, break, brush aside. Over and over I repeat this odd dance while the birds twitter in the trees above me. Are they enjoying my performance?

I come upon a massive web shaped like a bulls-eye that completely crosses the path. I am amazed at how wide a distance this spider has encompassed with its web; from a tree limb on one side of the path across 8 feet of open air to an anchor point in the tall grass on the other side of the path.

I stand and marvel at the feat required—how exactly does a small spider throw that first strand of thread across such a huge expanse? Does she fling herself from the tree branch into the abyss and hope for the best? Wait for just the right gust of wind? To me it seems truly miraculous that a small spider is able to create such a huge structure. Modern man would use thousands of dollars worth of sophisticated tools and not finish a structure of comparable scale for months. This spider did it in an hour or two.

Spiders never stop to consider that building a web 8 feet in diameter across open air is next to impossible. They just do it. Night after night, they jump off into the abyss and end up creating exquisite web masterpieces. It is as if they realize that this night and this web may be their last fling at greatness.

In contrast, I spend countless hours talking myself out of trying something that looks a little hard. I play it safe a lot. I rarely leap into the abyss and risk failure by trying something difficult. Maybe that's why I don't create the Taj Mahal or a literary masterpiece. I talk myself into safe mediocrity.

I want to be more like a spider; I want to fling myself into my writing body, heart and soul day after day. And maybe, just maybe, if I let myself dream big enough, I will create a single masterpiece before I die.

Months later, on a day when I am pushing and prodding myself to write a masterpiece RIGHT NOW, I discover an Osage Indian legend on an obscure web site. I find myself grinning from ear to ear as I read the legend—it is as thought the wise elders of the Osage tribe are sending me messages from beyond:

> One day, the chief of the Isolated Earth people was hunting in the forest. He was also hunting for a symbol to give life to his people. He came upon the tracks of a huge deer. The chief became very excited.
>
> "Grandfather Deer," he said, "surely you will show yourself to me. You are going to become the symbol of my people."
>
> He began to follow the tracks. His eyes were on nothing else as he followed those tracks, and he ran faster and faster through the forest. Suddenly, he ran right into a huge spider's web that had been strung between the trees, across the trail. When he got up, he was very angry. He struck at the spider who was sitting at the edge of the web. But the spider jumped out of reach. Then the spider spoke to the man.

"Grandson," the spider said, "why do you run through the woods looking at nothing but the ground?"

The chief felt foolish, but he had to answer the spider. "I was following the tracks of a great deer," the chief said. "I am seeking a symbol of strength for my people."

"I can be such a symbol", said the spider.

"How can you be a symbol of strength?" said the chief. "You are small and weak, and I didn't even see you as I followed the great Deer."

"Grandson," said the spider, "look upon me. I am patient. I watch and I wait. Then all things come to me. If your people learn this, they will be strong indeed."

The chief saw that this was so. Thus the Spider became one of the symbols of the people.

The Osage Indians called themselves Niu Konska—Little Ones of the Middle Waters. The Niu Konska believe they were born when the Sky People fell from the stars and joined with the Earth People to create their tribe. They lived and hunted on this land I now call home for a thousand years or more.

The Niu Konska were forced onto reservations in southern Kansas and Oklahoma in the early 1800's. The tribe now has a small reservation in northern Oklahoma.

Leap

Rocky is performing again. Rocky is a squirrel that lives on my hilltop—or actually any one of three squirrels that look so much alike I cannot tell them apart. Every day, Rocky performs a death-defying circus act on the back hill.

The back hill is covered with trees except for a cleared strip of grass running down the middle toward the pond. The grass strip is wide enough that the tree limbs arch up and over the grass, but do not quite touch each other in the middle. But two of the larger trees have limbs whose tiniest branches are within a foot or so of touching. And that is where Rocky does his high wire act.

Rocky manages to race from one edge of my back yard to the other without ever touching terra firma. He has discovered that those tiny branches that do not quite touch are just barely within leaping distance for him. Rocky does not even slow down when he approaches the gap. Instead he launches himself into the air and lands gracefully on the branch on the other side.

Rocky leaps the void 20 feet off the ground many times each day without a moment's hesitation. This act of bravery has earned him my admiration and the nickname "Rocky the Flying Squirrel". Actually, Rocky appears to be a rather average red squirrel. The woods around here are full of red squirrels. But oh, what a fearless leap he makes! Every time I witness it, I find myself holding my breath and praying for a safe landing. The distance Rocky leaps is astounding to me. Yet, I have never seen him fail. I wonder how he does it again and again.

One thing I have noticed is that Rocky does not sit and reflect on his death defying leap and his odds of making it. He just races up and does it. I could take a lesson from Rocky. I waste so much time worrying about whether I will fail at something that I yearn to try. I take my fear of failing at something and allow it to paralyze me. If I lived in the trees on the back hill, would I spend all my time cowering and worrying about falling? Maybe I should be more like this little squirrel and just go for it.

I want to leap into writing like Rocky the Flying Squirrel. To hell with failing or succeeding, just race up and launch myself into the void. Just give it my best shot. And know that somehow there will be a safe landing on the other side. Now that's faith.

Can I have that much faith in myself?

I am still toying with the idea of writing for a living. I am not certain exactly what that means. I just know I love the act of writing. Nothing can match the joy of feeling words flow out of my hand and onto the paper. Putting pen to paper is pure magic, like flying through the air with the greatest of ease. I become Nancy the Writer with Wings! Look out Rocky—here I go…

Write

Yesterday I walked my familiar pond path and pondered my future. What exactly is a "good living"? Is it my fate to manage computer system architects for 20 more years? The more successful I am in corporate America, the more I wonder if there is more to life than creating the most efficient computer network or being a respected manager.

I have been pondering a new word lately—dharma. Dharma is a Buddhist concept. It refers to the cosmic order of the Universe. Dharma is also used to describe human actions that maintain the cosmic order. Human dharma is defined as living in accordance with the basic rules that form and shape how the world works.

I look around me. I have walked this path through many years, through many seasons. Today tiny new leaves and buds greet me on every branch. The smell of awakening earth envelops me. Spring is here. I sense the order to the natural world around me. Seasons come and go. Plants leaf out, bloom, go to seed and then die back to rest for the winter.

Does a Redbud tree worry about how successful it will be, how many leaves it will grow, how many flowers and seedlings it will produce before it dies? No, a tree is too busy just being a tree. I spend so much time worrying about success and failure and what I am supposed to do—maybe I should just let go and be myself. Stop worrying about what the world will think and how much they will pay me.

What is my dharma? What actions can I take that help maintain the cosmic order of the Universe? I want my dharma to be rooted in the way I live each day. For me, dharma is about practicing the big truths of life, attempting to live from a place of integrity and love. And dharma is also about living my life from a mental and emotional space that honors the essence of who I am and what I bring to the world.

As I walk the pond path, I had a flash of memory: I am sitting in my 5th grade classroom. I close my eyes and see every detail of that classroom in my elementary school with its yellow cinder block walls and long dusty green chalkboard. I smell the chalk dust and feel the scarred wooden desktop beneath my fingertips.

That classroom is etched into my mind because of one event. Our assignment was to write 10 descriptive sentences. My teacher loved my outrageously descriptive sentences. And I loved her for loving my writing. I loved that assignment—I loved my teacher's praise, but most of all I loved the way I felt when I was writing. I felt gifted on that day. All was right with the Universe on that day.

I did not even voice my love of writing back then. No one would have understood. I did not understand it myself. The idea was too radical, too scary to acknowledge. My parents were raised during the depression. They carry scarred memories of ragged clothes and not enough to eat. They taught me that it was essential to go to college and get a degree so that I could get a well-paying stable job. It was the American dream—the true path to success and eternal happiness.

That vision of success and happiness effectively eliminated writing as a potential career for me before I even considered it. I understood writers to be flaky, unstable, immature dreamers without a practical bone in their bodies. They were starving artists living in cold, ugly apartments and scraping for every meal. I grew up hearing about how well engineering jobs paid. And accounting. And medicine. So, I went to college. And I worked hard and earned not one but three degrees. Never mind that many of the subjects that filled my brain bored me to tears. I wanted to make a good living, didn't I? Writers ended up starving and homeless, shivering in a cardboard box beneath the Broadway Bridge.

But today I took the leap despite my fears—I quit my job. I am officially a crazy, unstable, unemployed writer now. I am filled with joy, excitement—and sheer terror. I may be broke and hungry in a few months, but right now I cannot stop smiling.

It took this still place on a magical hilltop to open me up to the still sacred space within me. And nestled in my still sacred place, I found my pen and my voice.

So much of life is unclear, uncertain. Who knows where I will be in 20 years? But I know for certain that I love to write. I live to write. At my core I am a writer. The rest is window dressing. After years of peering into myself on this quiet hilltop, I finally understand that putting pen to paper is my dharma.

It has been a wild and wonderful journey in this space with only pen and pad to guide me. I cannot wait to see what's next.

Epilogue—Leaving the Nest

"Happiness is not a destination. It is the attitude with which you choose to travel."
—Yogi Arit Desal

It is 4 years since I left my corporate job and "became" a writer. I have written thousands of lines and even published a few.

And now another part of my life is transforming. Life is changing whether I am ready or not. My husband has been offered a job in Chicago. It is a wonderful job in the city where I was born. And just a few weeks before his fateful job offer, I learned that the woods and meadow next to my land had been purchased. A new house will soon take the place of old oak trees and wildflowers. Bulldozers reshape the hill as I write this. The Universe is telling me that it is time to move on. It is a lesson in the impermanence of life. Nothing can stay the same forever.

I am moving. I am moving! I shake my head in disbelief and repeat that phrase once, twice, ten times a day. I am leaving this house that I thought would be mine until I died. How could this happen? My mind is reeling with the logistics involved in selling one house, buying another and moving my family 600 miles away to a new state. It all makes my head spin. I head outside to walk the old familiar pond path. I need to clear my mind and find a little peace.

I walk my path and look around with a mix of sorrow and excitement; I am moving to a brand new place! But how will I leave this one behind? I have owned a lot of different houses, from small town to suburbia to country. But this hilltop is my hands down favorite. This little plot of land has opened my heart wide. I have grown to love my space here.

I walked through the rooms of the house last night remembering…my son picking out "big boy" dinosaur wallpaper for his room at the ripe old age of three. Now he says that same wallpaper is "for babies". My baby daughter was born in the master bedroom on a stormy night in October—the same bedroom that my partner and I created from ugly, unused space—the bedroom that we lovingly nicknamed our nest.

In reality the entire hilltop has been my nest. In this sheltered space I learned to trust my intuition. In this place I found the courage to quit my "important" corporate job and live off savings for years while I dug in my journal and slowly uncovered what makes my heart sing and why I am here on this Earth. In this quiet nest I learned to write again—a gift that has proven to be more precious than gold to me.

Now it is time to pack up my journal and pen and take wing to a new place. I honestly never thought I would leave this place. The trees whisper to me as I walk by, "It is time—fly away—it is time." I stop on the dock and look back up the hill. It is spring, my favorite season on this hill.

The trees are bursting with new buds. The birds are in full voice, wooing mates from every bush and tree. New grass sprinkles the slope tender green. I adore this hilltop—every stone, every leaf, every ripple on the pond. But it is time to go. I know it is. I feel it in my bones. It is time to move on.

I struggle to find a way to say good bye to this place that has sheltered me. It seems impossible. But as I turn to go, I smile through my tears. I realize that this place will be with me wherever I may travel. This sacred still space inhabits my heart.

About the Author

Nancy Lankston has worked as a computer analyst, Registered Nurse, teacher, research assistant and energetic healer. She holds degrees in Biology, Nursing and Computer Science. Nancy now lives with her family in the Midwest where she divides her time between writing and a private healing practice. Her favorite pastime continues to be writing prose and poetry about nature and spirituality.

More of Nancy's writing can be found at www.nancylankston.com

978-0-595-37757-2
0-595-37757-2

www.ingramcontent.com/pod-product-compliance
Lightning Source LLC
Chambersburg PA
CBHW020350290526
45785CB00005B/2215